Shetland Ponies

Story and Photographs

by LILO HESS

One May morning a farmer led two Shetland ponies away from the herd to a secluded pasture. Here their foals were born, and here through the spring and summer months they grew and learned.

Lilo Hess's sensitive camera followed the foals as they confronted first their mothers, then their surroundings, and finally each other. We see the new-born Blaze stagger to her feet for the first time, and later watch Patch in his comic encounters with a mud puddle and a feed pail.

The ponies' exploration of the world around them is described in warm, affectionate text and photographs. As we watch these gay, charming animals learning to eat and play, we see how distinct are their personalities: Patch romping, and adventurous; Blaze cautious and docile.

By the end of summer, when the ponies have rejoined the herd, we know them as individuals and realize why children everywhere love the playful, intelligent Shetland pony.

Shetland Ponies

Shetland Ponies

STORY AND PHOTOGRAPHS

by Lilo Hess

THOMAS Y. CROWELL COMPANY · NEW YORK

By Lilo Hess
Rabbits in the Meadow
Shetland Ponies

By Lilo Hess and Dorothy Childs Hogner
Odd Pets

The author acknowledges with thanks the cooperation of the owners of the Van B Pony Farm of Bath, Pennsylvania.

On A MILD MORNING in May a Shetland pony, named Shelly, looked out the barn door. Before her the fresh green fields glistened in the bright sun.

The mare was restless. She snorted and stamped her small hoofs. After a long winter the new grass looked inviting. But the bottom half of the barn door was closed and the pony could not get out.

Another pony stood dozing in the corner of the barn. Her name was Redwing. The farmer had separated them from the pony herd the night before and left them in the barn.

Both ponies were small and sturdy. They had cream-colored manes and tails. Shelly was silver-dapple, a silvery gray with white spots; and Redwing was a beautiful sorrel, or reddish brown, with white spots. Each was expecting a foal.

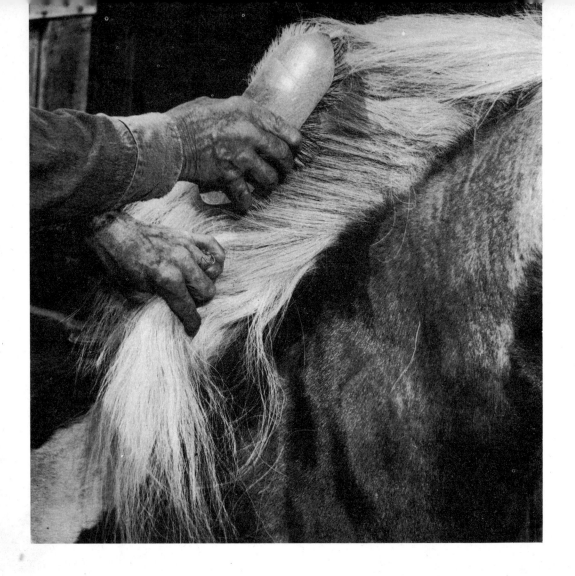

A truck pulled up to the stable door and the farmer got out. He had a brush and currycomb in his hand and started to brush the small horses. Shelly and Redwing pushed each other and nudged the farmer to attract his attention.

They enjoyed being brushed. Their shaggy winter

2

fur was loose and the farmer combed it out with the strong, blunt teeth of the currycomb. He brushed their manes, tangled by the wind, until they were smooth.

When he finished he led the ponies up a ramp into the truck. Shelly balked at the strange truck. The farmer had to tie her securely.

He drove up a narrow, woodsy road in back of his farm. At the end of the road was an enclosed pasture into which he led the ponies. At one end of the pasture was a small shelter. The farmer fastened a bucket in each corner of the shelter and filled each of them with corn and oats. He put a bale of hay on the rack. Then he patted the ponies and drove away.

Shelly and Redwing explored their new home. There was a small wood for shade when the sun got too warm, and a field for grazing. A high wire fence ran all around.

It was still and peaceful, but the ponies did not know solitude. They had lived all winter with a large herd and were used to a barn with a big hayrack. At feeding time the ponies had galloped into the barn, pushing and kicking each other in a friendly way.

Now Shelly and Redwing had all the hay and grain they wanted, but no friends. They stamped their hoofs in protest. Finally they ate some new grass and then they fell asleep standing up.

In this quiet spot they could have plenty of rest and good food. When their foals were born, no harm would come to them.

The next day the farmer came to feed them and give them fresh water. When he left, they were alone again in the quiet field.

Their mother and father had come from the Shetland Islands, north of Scotland, where the climate was wet and cold. There ponies ate the sour grass of the marshes or the few weeds they could find on the rocky island. They were always hungry. There were no shelters, and the stormy winds tossed their long manes and tails. The "Shelties," as the islanders called the ponies, were tough and sturdy, but they never grew as big as other horses.

No one knows where the ponies came from, or how they got to the island. They have been there as long as people can remember.

About the middle of the nineteenth century Shetland ponies were brought to England for the first time. Children liked them because they were gay, gentle, and small. Soon they became known all over the world. Horse dealers went to the islands, rounded up the ponies, and shipped them to many countries.

Several years ago the farmer bought a stallion and a mare. Their first foal was Redwing and then a year later Shelly was born.

Still later the farmer bought another stallion called Toy. He was reddish gold and had a long, white mane and tail.

Toy's coat was brushed and curried every day and the farmer took him out to graze on a long lead rope. He became the father of Shelly's and Redwing's foals.

In the pasture Redwing walked back and forth. She was very restless and pawed the ground with her hoofs. She put her nose down to sniff the cool soil. Toward evening she found a spot she liked and fell asleep there. Shelly watched but did not go near her.

In the morning Redwing's foal was born. It was a girl, a filly. She lay limply on the ground. First Redwing licked and cleaned her. Then she nudged her gently to make her stand up. But the filly's hind legs were weak and she fell back to the ground.

She lay still and probably would have fallen asleep,
but Redwing neighed loudly. The filly jumped up and
this time her legs held steady.

12

She was a sorrel like her mother with a white blaze on her forehead. She had large, soft eyes and fuzzy, pointed ears. The more Redwing licked her fur, the curlier it got.

The little one pressed close to Redwing's side, for she liked the warmth and nearness of her mother. After a while Redwing moved away.

14

She wanted her child to follow, but the filly did not understand. Redwing turned and pushed her gently. Finally she gave a loud whinny and the frightened filly ran a few steps in the wrong direction. Redwing quickly went after her and nipped her with her teeth. Now the filly understood she had to do what her mother wanted. She followed Redwing to the edge of the wood. There the little one rested and Redwing stood watch. Shelly looked at the new baby; but every time she approached, Redwing showed her teeth and snorted in an angry way.

When the little filly awoke she got up and peeped shyly from behind her mother. At first she did not know how to get her milk.

Redwing nudged her toward the udder. Then she
eagerly sucked the warm milk. Already the baby
seemed to have grown. The tight curls in her fur had
vanished and only a few loose waves remained.

In the evening Redwing went to the pasture to graze and the filly stayed close by her side. Later, they settled down for the night in a corner of the enclosure. Redwing silently watched and listened, always ready to flee into the wood if danger came.

When the farmer arrived the next morning, the filly was scared and wanted to run away. But she saw her mother walk up to be petted and came forward slowly. Then, as if startled by her own boldness, she bounded away. Redwing trotted after her, bumped her roughly, and made her go back. Because of the white marking on her forehead, the farmer named her Blaze.

Blaze went with her mother to drink at the water trough. Her first mouthful surprised her and she blew it out through her nostrils. Then she tried again, liked it, and drank deeply.

Now Shelly got more and more restless. She paced up and down and ate very little. The next morning she, too, was a mother. Her foal was a boy, or colt. By daybreak he was standing up and soon he was gaily jumping around. He was a very sure-footed baby.

He had a well-shaped head and a rust-brown coat with white patches. When the farmer saw him, he named him Patch.

Patch was very different from Blaze. He was not at all shy or quiet. He could not stand still for long, but liked to kick his heels and run.

22

Shelly could hardly keep up with him. She had to bump and nip him often to make him behave. It was several days before he learned to follow her.

Each mother kept her foal as far from the other as possible. Sometimes Blaze would look curiously at Patch, but she was afraid to go near him.

Slowly the days passed. Blaze learned to run and jump, but usually she stayed close to her mother. She nibbled hay and grass, although milk was all she really needed. She knew how to clean herself and scratch her ear with her hind foot without toppling over.

Patch did not do anything for himself. His mother cleaned him when she could catch him standing still. Afterward he leaped into the air and kicked his legs. Sometimes he jumped up against his mother. When he was out of breath he rested for a few minutes and then started over again.

26

The foals, now almost four weeks old, still paid no attention to each other. When their mothers went to the shelter to feed, they never looked at each other.

One day Patch wandered into the wood, as he often did. Suddenly he saw something move in the dry leaves. It was a snake. Patch went closer and closer.

Redwing saw him first and neighed a shrill alarm.
Patch heard her and stopped. Then Shelly screamed
and ran between her foal and the snake. She pushed
him back roughly. The snake quickly slid under a log.
A bit shaken, Patch stayed beside his mother for the
rest of the day.

The weeks went by and the foals became more independent. Once, while running, they suddenly bumped heads. They looked surprised. They sniffed each other. Then they started to play together.

Patch nipped Blaze and reared up on his hind legs. She jumped into the air and kicked her heels. Every time she stopped, Patch bumped her with his nose. He wanted her to keep playing. They became good friends.

The foals started to eat the long grass in the field. They grazed side by side, while their mothers watched them. Sometimes Blaze dug up the sod with her tiny hoofs and licked the soil.

When she felt happy she lay down and rolled over and over, rubbing her back against the cool grass.

A black squirrel liked to come to the pony shelter and pick up fallen grains of oats and corn. Usually it came when the ponies were away. But once Blaze unexpectedly returned to the shelter when the squirrel was there. For a second the squirrel sat still as a statue. The filly let out a sharp squeal. Then both bolted away.

But this time Blaze did not run to her mother for protection. She ran to her friend Patch. He started to nip and tease her and Blaze soon forgot her fear. With a burst of speed the foals raced over the meadow, their manes and tails flying.

The summer slowly came to an end. Blaze looked and acted more grown-up. Her fur was smoother and her mane had turned lighter. Patch had changed very little. He still spent most of his time kicking his heels and running. When he did not like something he flared his nostrils and butted the nearest object with his head.

35

Once after a rainstorm Patch found a big mud puddle and rolled in it. When he got up he looked like a different pony. He was mud-gray all over. The mud dried and caked on his warm body. It pulled his skin tight and he felt uncomfortable. He rubbed against the walls of the shelter. He jumped angrily up and down.

Suddenly in a burst of rage he stuck his head deep into his mother's feed bucket. He shook his head so hard that the bucket came off its hook.

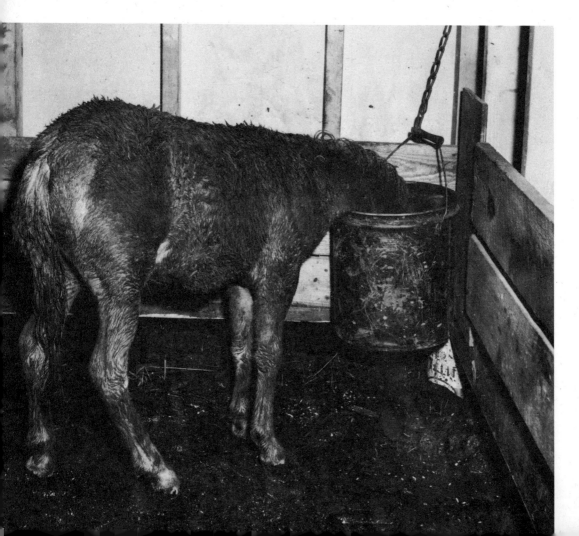

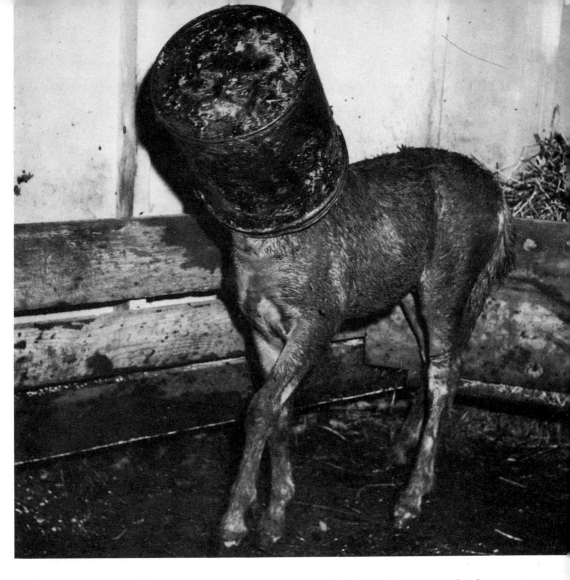

Inside the bucket it was dark and Patch squealed
like a baby. The other ponies paid no attention. He
shook his head sideways. Nothing happened. Finally
he shook his head up and down and the bucket fell off.
Patch was lucky. The rain started again and the mud
washed off.

Early one morning the farmer brought his truck to the pasture. He snapped lead ropes on Shelly's and Redwing's halters and led them into the truck.

Then he slipped a small halter over Blaze's head. When he started to pull, Blaze balked and dug in her heels. The farmer had to push her into the truck.

Patch went in without protest. The farmer drove the ponies back to the herd.

Other mares with their foals were back also. When the farmer opened the truck, Blaze and Patch were frightened and would not come down. Their mothers trotted down the ramp and sniffed the familiar smells.

When the other ponies saw the new arrivals they galloped toward them. The mares neighed and trumpeted noisily. The foals bleated. Blaze and Patch rushed down the ramp and hid behind their mothers.

40

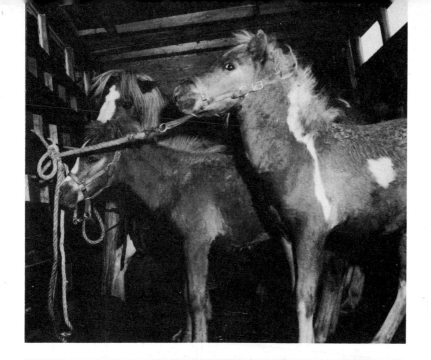

The farmer quickly tied Redwing and Shelly to the
fence. Then he waved his arms and shooed the other
ponies away. Next he took Redwing on a lead rope to

42

meet the ponies. They circled her, sniffing. After a few minutes they lost interest. The farmer did the same with Shelly and soon it was peaceful again at the pony farm.

Blaze found a new friend right away. It was Blacky, the barnyard cat. She followed Blacky until the cat got tired of her and vanished under the fence.

At first Shelly and Redwing kept their foals away from the herd. Patch and his mother grazed and explored the rolling hills of the farm. Redwing led Blaze to a nearby stream. The filly had never seen so much water before and would not go in. She trotted along the shore, as Redwing waded upstream.

Suddenly two frisky ponies ran toward her. Frightened, Blaze jumped into the water to be near her mother. Now that she was wet, she seemed to like the water and splashed happily in it.

46

When evening came Redwing and Shelly led their foals to an old apple tree. Many ponies were eating the fallen fruit. Redwing and Shelly approached cautiously, but the ponies paid no attention to them. The herd had accepted them again.

Early next morning the farmer took Shelly and Redwing and their foals to the stables. There he brushed and curried them and trimmed their hoofs.

From a nearby stall came a loud whinny and a handsome pony peered out the door. It was Toy, the father of Patch and Blaze. Blaze walked toward him. They looked at each other and rubbed their soft noses together. Patch watched with interest but did not go near the stallion.

In the afternoon Blaze made new friends. She was asleep in the pasture when two mares and a foal approached. Blaze wanted to run away, but the ponies seemed friendly. They sniffed her and stayed near her until she went back to sleep.

Fall was coming. The air grew colder. Soon the leaves looked as if they were splashed with red and yellow paint. The grass became dry and the ponies roamed farther and farther to search for tender blades.

Redwing usually led the herd out of the barn in the morning. Blaze no longer stayed close to her. She liked the company of the other foals, although Patch was still her special friend.

Every fall the farmer invited his friends to see the new foals. He put halters on the ponies and showed them one by one. At the end his guests voted for the foal they liked best.

This year Blaze got the prize. The farmer pinned a red ribbon on her. But Blaze wanted only to go back to her mother.

Redwing waited for her in the pasture. As soon as Blaze was with her again she led her away from the people. The filly was very hungry after all the excitement and hurried to drink her mother's milk. Soon she would eat only oats, corn, grass, and hay. Then she would be weaned.

The days were getting shorter. Winter drew near.
The ponies' fur was very long. They had grown their
winter coats and looked shaggy and warm.

One night it snowed and the next morning frost
sparkled in the ponies' manes. The foals had never seen
snow before.

Some licked the cold white flakes, some rolled in it. Patch kicked his heels and jumped, but Blaze just looked surprised. Later the sun came out and melted the snow quickly.

There would be more snow on the hills of the pony farm. Blaze and Patch would get used to it. They would eat the hay and grain the farmer gave them. When the weather grew too cold they would stay close together in the warm barn.

They had many new friends to play with during the long winter. Then spring with its green grass and warm sunshine would come again.

57

About the Author

Lilo Hess was born in Germany and attended school there and in England and Switzerland. Her studies included zoology and photography, and she has combined these interests in her profession, animal photography. The Pennsylvania countryside is the background for Miss Hess as she observes and photographs the birth and life of wood and field animals.

Miss Hess is a member of the American Society of Magazine Photographers, and her pictures of animals have appeared in innumerable American and European publications.